Clean

The Journal

DOUGLAS WEISS, PHD

Clean

The Journal

Contents:

A Dirty War Declared

As men, all of us are sexual creatures. We are all created sexual in the image of our God. Remember, Adam was created as a sexual man way before Eve was conceived or created by God.

There's no scene in Genesis chapter 2 where God endows Adam with sex organs now that he was going to create Eve. Rather, God created man like all mammals to "go forth and multiply." We, like Adam, all had a season of being sexual, but not being aware of it.

Take a moment and remember when you were a child, or even a teenager, and try to remember when you were not aware of sexuality. Some of you remember when girls were icky and not anyone you might want to share time with. Now, take a moment and write down a memory of a time when you were oblivious to being in a sexual world.

_____

_____

_____

Then it happened; each one of us had our own unique experience of becoming sexually aware. For some it was a girl kissing you; for others it was a peer telling you stories or unfortunately an older boy showing you his dad's magazines. Some were violated in their first sexual awareness by a male or female predator.

All of us have a story to tell about when we first became aware of sexual attractiveness or sexuality. Take a second and think about yourself when sexual awareness or sexuality came into your life story? What did you think or feel when sexuality occurred. For some, this was a positive awakening; for others the enemy tainted even your sexual awakening with guilt or shame.

In the below space, write out your awakening. Then how you felt or what you thought about this.

My awakening was: _____

_____

_____

_____

My thoughts and feelings were: _____

_____

_____

_____

For most, but not all men, the enemy who fears you attempted to declare the dirty war in your life. The devil doesn't wait until you're a fully equipped man of God. He attacks you as a child or adolescent because he is, above all things, a coward preying on the weak.

The dirty war starts in so many different ways as future men of God. I have listened to men for more than twenty years tell their tales of when the war was declared on them sexually. For some it was sexually inappropriate thoughts about people around them. Other men were moved by sexual fantasies of real or unreal people such as individuals on television, in movies, magazines or even comic books.

A significant group of men are thrown the grenade of pornography or nudity even in National Geographic, photo magazines, nude decks of cards or Playboy, and now we have a real venomous weapon from the enemy called the Internet.

Think back again. When did the enemy declare war on you sexually? How did he organize it so that you would be exposed to sexuality in an ungodly way? How has this impacted you? Write down the answer to these questions and be specific.

1. How did the enemy declare war on you sexually?

_____

_____

_____

2. How did he organize it so that you would be exposed to sexuality in an ungodly way?

_____

_____

_____

3. How has this impacted you?

_____

_____

_____

When one nation or kingdom declares war on another, there is almost always more than just the first conflict. The first conflict is just the beginning of the war. There are often many other battles that occur until the war is finally over. In Christ, we can ultimately win. However, it can be helpful to look back over a few of the significant battles you have won and others that you may have lost. You and I can learn from our own battles as well as the others.

In the below spaces write out three examples of sexual battles you know you were the victor in. Give examples of real temptations that you escaped or overcame.

1. _____

_____

_____

2. _____

_____

_____

3. _____

_____

Here, I want you to acknowledge sexual battles or rounds that if a referee was looking, he would have given that round to the enemy. He tempted you, or maybe you tempted you, and you lost by any standard.

1. _____

_____

_____

2. _____

_____

_____

3. _____

_____

_____

This part of this journal is to get you to see sexuality in God's image. Most of us have had a season of sexual innocence. All of us have had some sexual awakening between innocence and violations. Almost all of us have had war declared on us by the enemy who is afraid of us. Lastly, most of us have won and lost some battles.

Share your findings in this journey you have taken together with some brothers. If you are doing this in a group, which I hope you are, break up into smaller groups and walk through this together. You will be amazed at what you learn from each other.

Date I shared these findings of my journey was: _____

Now let us turn to some of the statistics you read about pornography in the chapter, A Dirty War Declared.

What are your thoughts about time spent on pornography? _____

_____

_____

What are your thoughts about money spent on pornography? _____

_____

_____

What are your thoughts about America leading the world in porn development and distribution?

_____

_____

What does it mean to you that women are increasingly being entrapped by pornography? _____

_____

What does it mean to you that clergy are getting trapped in pornography?

_____

_____

What do you think some of the possible impacts would be on a church whose leaders are trapped in pornography?

1. _____

2. _____

3. _____

4. _____

What does it mean to you that "your people" (Christian men) are viewing pornography? _____

_____

What does it mean to you that Christian children are viewing pornography?

_____

_____

_____

If you have children at home, what can you do to limit their access to pornography in their lives?

1. _____

2. _____

3. _____

4. _____

As a Christian man, how has reading through these statistics impacted you?

_____

_____

_____

_____

Have you ever heard of God recognizing a nation as clean or unclean based on its immorality?

Yes_____   No_____

What are your thoughts about God's perspective on America, your state, city or church?

_____

_____

_____

_____

Take a moment to pray and ask the Lord what are actions He would have you take. Record these below.

1. _____

2. _____

3. _____

4. _____

5. _____

The date you shared your answers with another man was: _____

Your Destiny is Waiting

Many of you have been walking with the Lord for many years. I, myself, have had many spiritual leaders in my life, just as you may have. Take a moment and list by initial (T.J. for Tom Jones) all of the spiritual leaders you have had that have fallen to sexual sin.

_____   _____   _____   _____

_____   _____   _____   _____

_____   _____   _____   _____

Half of the pastors of churches I've attended have fallen into sexual sin. Over three decades as a Christian, I have seen what this has done to their professional and personal life and how it has affected the lives of others. Using the same initials write out briefly what has happen to their lives.

1. _____ : _____

2. _____ : _____

3. _____ : _____

4. _____: _____

5. _____: _____

6. _____: _____

7. _____: _____

8. _____: _____

9. _____: _____

10. _____: _____

What have you learned from real life examples involving sex and destiny?

_____

_____

_____

_____

What are the lessons you take away from Joseph's refusal to participate in sexual sin with Potiphar's wife?

1. _____

2. _____

3. _____

What are the lessons you take away from Samson's fall into sexual temptation?

1. _____

2. _____

3. _____

What does the phrase, "Your freedom isn't just about you," mean to you?

_____

_____

_____

_____

Before God created Adam, God had a purpose for Adam to tend the Garden.
Before God created Eve, He created her purpose, to be man's helpmate. Both
purposes were solutions to a problem on earth.

God took a long time creating your purpose before he placed you in your
mother's womb. Your purpose was created before you were made. Your gifts
are aligned with your purpose.

What do you understand about the phrase, "You are God's solution for
someone or something on earth."?

_____

_____

_____

_____

If you have figured out what solution(s) you bring to others in the world, write them down.

1. _____

2. _____

3. _____

4. _____

I want you to think for a moment about your destiny. What is the destiny that Christ has made for you? Quiet yourself, close your eyes and ask Him what your destiny is. Write your answer below.

_____

_____

_____

_____

How would the world be different if you reached your destiny?

_____

_____

_____

_____

How would the lives of people around you be different if you arrived at your destiny?

_____

_____

_____

_____

Has the devil in the past laid sexual traps to try to keep you from your destiny? If so, briefly explain below.

1. _____

2. _____

3. _____

4. _____

5. _____

Currently is there a sexual temptation or situation that the enemy has orchestrated to keep you from your destiny? If so, write it down.

_____

_____

_____

_____

If you have a current situation, what can you plan to do to be successful?

_____

_____

_____

_____

What does the statement mean to you that sexual temptation is too small for you?

_____

_____

_____

_____

What are the most important things you have learned from this chapter?

_____

_____

_____

_____

What is the date you shared your answers with another man? _____

Authority at Stake

As a man, knowing the why behind doing something makes it significantly easier to persevere through a process. Give a few examples where knowing why helped you persevere through something in your life.

1. _____

2. _____

3. _____

What do you now think about the statement, "sexual temptation has absolutely nothing to do with sex at all."?

_____

_____

_____

_____

When you think of the word tolerate what do you think about?

_____

_____

_____

_____

Explain the difference between God being patient, but not tolerant.

_____

_____

_____

_____

As a young boy, if you had a dad or other consistent male figure present, what were some of the few things this man would not tolerate from you?

1. _____

2. _____

3. _____

What would happen to you if you did the things that this man would not tolerate?

1. _____

2. _____

3. _____

How do you think Jezebel spun being sexually immoral as acceptable to her local church?

1. _____

2. _____

3. _____

Tolerating something often means you just become silent about it. If I am going to tolerate my child not cleaning their room or using profanity, I would just be quiet about the matter. Of the churches you have been in, how would you rate them and why on being tolerant of the sexual misbehaviors of its church members.

_____

_____

_____

_____

How do you interpret Hebrews 13:8 about God being the same yesterday, today and forever when it comes to sexual sin?

_____

_____

_____

_____

When you hear the statement, "Jezebel hasn't changed. Her spirit has the same goal: seduce you then reduce you," what does it mean to you?

_____

_____

_____

_____

Give a real life example (you don't need to name the person) of when someone has been seduced and reduced. What happened to seduce them and how have they been reduced?

Seduced: _____

_____

_____

_____

Reduced: _____

_____

_____

_____

Why do you think the enemy of the church and your soul has made so much pornography available and in many cases for free?

_____

_____

_____

_____

A drug dealer peddling drugs to potential clients has a script or lure, and seduces people into trying it at least once. What do you think would be the devil's pitch or lines to seduce Christian men into looking at pornography?

1. _____

2. _____

3. _____

Which line in the past has the enemy used to seduce you into sexual temptation or pornography?

_____

_____

_____

_____

How is your thinking different from Jezebel's doctrine that said, "You could be a Christian, sleep around and do sexually whatever you wanted."? She certainly taught that individuals were in charge of their sexuality, not God, and they were free to do as they pleased.

_____

_____

_____

_____

God has sown patience with Jezebel and He had, "given her time to repent." Give examples of God giving you time to repent of something.

1. _____

2. _____

3. _____

Are there areas in your life, sexual or not, that like Jezebel, you are unwilling to repent? If so, write them down.

1. _____

2. _____

3. _____

In the portion of Scripture in Revelation 2, it talks about a "bed of suffering." This would probably be the worst things that could happen to you or to those you love dearly. In your own mind, if the worst possible things were to happen to you, what would they be?

1. _____

2. _____

3. _____

What do you think about when you read all of the different and creative ways God stepped into someone's life to expose their sexual sin?

_____

_____

_____

_____

Have you ever thought about the Scripture in context (Rev. 2) where Jesus says, "I will strike her children dead."?

     Yes_____   No_____

Looking at this, what do you think about who Jesus is and how He feels about sexual duplicity in believers?

_____

_____

_____

_____

What is Satan's "deep secret"?

_____

_____

_____

_____

What would it mean for you to have authority over anything?

_____

_____

_____

_____

What does it mean to you that your DNA is to have authority over nations?

_____

_____

_____

_____

After reading this chapter, what is really at stake in this sexual battle for you and Christian men everywhere?

_____

_____

_____

_____

If your gifts and abilities were able to impact multiple nations, how would the world be a different place?

_____

_____

_____

_____

If you started to use your gifts now at home, in your local church, and community, how would each of these be different?

Home: _____

_____

Church: _____

_____

Community: _____

_____

The most important things I have learned from this chapter are:

_____

_____

_____

_____

The date you shared your answers with another man was: _____

Carry Your Weapons

One of the greatest gifts we receive in this life is to watch the lives of those around us. I have been blessed in so many ways to have learned from others who have done well in life and I also have learned by others through their mistakes.

Learning from others is an essential ingredient in wisdom. If I can learn from others I can expedite my own life choices in a more positive and informed manner.

As you read Joe's story, what were some of the things you learned that could be helpful so that you don't make the same mistakes. List them below.

1. _____

2. _____

3. _____

When you hear the statement, "stupidity meets opportunity" what do you think about?

_____

_____

_____

_____

As a man, what does (or will) it mean to you that you are (or will be) married to God's daughter?

_____

_____

_____

_____

What does it really mean to you that God is (or will be) your Father-in-law?

_____

_____

_____

_____

Joe hit a point where his secret was exposed. How do you think it felt for Joe to go tell his wife again?

_____

_____

_____

Do you think God is committed to expose any of your sexual secrets because He loves you? Why?

_____

_____

_____

_____

Why does God give you a spiritual sword?

_____

_____

_____

_____

What is the limitation of a sword?

_____

_____

_____

_____

According to James 1:15, what are the three stages of the seed of lust?

1. Lust
2. _____
3. _____

Lust is A_____ W_____ ac-
cording to Exodus 20:17.

What women, according to Jesus' interpretation of a neighbor, are we not
allowed to lust after?

_____

_____

_____

_____

What is the difference between seeing a woman as a person or an object?

Person _____

_____

_____

_____

Object _____

_____

_____

When a man fertilizes lust, he G _____ the seed to grow to the next stage.

What are the ways a man can fertilize lust?

1. _____

2. _____

3. _____

4. _____

5. _____

6. _____

What would be examples of each stage of lust?

Lust: _____

_____

Sin: _____

_____

Death: _____

_____

In your own words, explain the key points of a man with a dropped sword.

1. Has never committed to be clean: _____

_____

2. No plan: _____

_____

3. No boundaries: _____

_____

4. Not honest or accountable: _____

_____

In your own words, explain the key points of a man with an armed sword:
1. Commit to be clean: _____

_____

2. They have a plan: _____

_____

3. Honest and accountable: _____

_____

4. Consequences: _____

_____

After examining the models of the dropped and armed sword, which do you currently have and why?

_____

_____

_____

_____

How do you think family and church members feel around a man with a dropped sword?

Family Feels: _____

_____

Church Members Feel: _____

_____

How do you think family and church members feel around a man with an armed sword?

Family Feels: _____

_____

Church Members Feel: _____

_____

In detail, write out your plan to have an armed sword.

_____

_____

_____

_____

When and where did you commit to be clean? If you don't have a place and time, make it now.

Time and place I committed to be clean was: _____

My plan to be clean is:

_____

_____

_____

_____

I will be honest and accountable to:

Who: _____

When: _____

About What: _____

Consequences

The behaviors I will have consequences for are:

1. _____   6. _____

2. _____   7. _____

3. _____   8. _____

4. _____   9. _____

5. _____   10. _____

My consequences for these behaviors are:

Behavior	Consequence 1st Time	2nd Time	3rd Time

1. _____

2. _____

3. _____

4. _____

5. _____

6. _____

7. _____

8. _____

9. _____

10. _____

The most important things I have learned from this chapter are:

_____

_____

_____

_____

The date you shared your answers with another man was: _____

U + P = D

This chapter takes you down a road that most of you have never travelled. This is a road that highlights the various impacts of pornography, not on you, but on those around you. To start, we discussed the principle of cause and effect.

When you hear the term cause and effect, what are some images that come into your mind?

1. _____

2. _____

3. _____

Explain some cause and effect principles that you have discovered over the course of your life.

1. _____

2. _____

3. _____

4. _____

5. _____

How are a fireplace and a marriage similar according to this chapter?

_____

_____

_____

_____

With whom is God's only perfect sexual will for your life?

_____

In the below spaces, write out each word for the formula U + P = D

U_____

P_____

D_____

What are your thoughts about pornography lowering the self-esteem of the wife of the man who views pornography?

_____

_____

_____

_____

What are your thoughts about how a man viewing pornography increases the symptoms of depression in his wife?

_____

_____

_____

_____

What are your thoughts about pornography viewing impacting a wife's weight?

_____

_____

_____

_____

What are your thoughts about a man who participates in a behavior that can cause his wife's esteem to lower, weight to go higher and cause depression?

_____

_____

_____

In this chapter you were exposed to statistics that demonstrate the direct impact of a man's pornography usage on his wife. In Scripture we are told that a husband and wife become one flesh. What do you conclude from a man's pornography viewing and sexual sin as its impacts his wife?

_____

_____

_____

_____

I heard a pastor once say that there is no such thing as a secret. What are your thoughts when you look at the statistic where 67% of the children found out about their dad's or parents' sexual inappropriate behavior by the age 18?

_____

_____

_____

_____

Did you have an experience where you found out about a parent's pornography or sexually inappropriate materials or behaviors? If so, explain what happened.

_____

_____

_____

In this chapter you were exposed to eighteen areas of impact that affected adult children of men who acted out sexually inappropriately with porn and other activities. These categories of impact included:

Self-Esteem	Romantic Relationships
Spiritually	Sexual Beliefs
Socially	Sexual Addiction
Dating	Depression
Emotionally	Sexual Choices
Marriage	Financially
Marital Relationships	Parenting
Morally	Eating Disorders
Financial Life	Sexual Anorexia

What are your thoughts about a man's pornography viewing and other sexual behaviors impacting his children?

_____

_____

_____

_____

What do you think of a man who knowingly creates damage in a variety of areas for his children?

_____

_____

_____

_____

The number one lie I hear from Christen men viewing pornography or acting out sexually with themselves or others is, "It's not hurting anybody." In the below space, write the names of people that would be impacted by your sexual purity or your sexual impurity.

1. _____	11. _____	21. _____
2. _____	12. _____	22. _____
3. _____	13. _____	23. _____
4. _____	14. _____	24. _____
5. _____	15. _____	25. _____
6. _____	16. _____	25. _____
7. _____	17. _____	26. _____
8. _____	18. _____	27. _____
9. _____	19. _____	29. _____
10. _____	20. _____	30. _____

In the below space, write down the legacy you want the following people to be able to honestly say at your funeral.

My Wife _____

_____

_____

My Children _____

_____

_____

My Siblings _____

_____

_____

My Coworkers _____

_____

_____

My Pastor _____

_____

_____

My Friends _____

_____

_____

We all have a legacy and are impacting all the people around us. My prayer is that all Christian men can have the clean legacy Christ has purchased for us.

The most important things I have learned from this chapter are:

_____

_____

_____

_____

The date you shared your answers with another man was: _____

Clean Brain

In this chapter, I share with you the game of peek-a-boo that God played with me. He kept having me read a Scripture over and over and then one day He gave me real revelation on its meaning. Can you give an example when God gave you a real revelation on a Scripture?

Yes_____   No_____

If yes, briefly write down what God showed you.

_____

_____

_____

_____

What is your second largest sex organ?

_____

When you have sex, your brain receives the mother lode of E_____ and E_____.

In your own words, describe sexual impurity:

_____

_____

_____

_____

In your own words describe a landmine:

_____

_____

_____

_____

Now that you understand what a landmine is, be honest and ask yourself if you have created landmines in your younger years or currently? If you have, are you clear on what these landmines are?

Yes_____   No_____

If yes, you would do well to discuss this with another man or in your group. Once you share this, you can have more support, if a landmine comes across your path.

In your own words, describe emotional landmines:

_____

_____

_____

_____

Now that you understand what an emotional landmine is, be honest and ask yourself if you have created emotional landmines in your younger years or currently? If you have, are you clear on what these emotional landmines are?

Yes_____   No_____

If yes, you would do well to discuss this with another man or in your group. Once you share this you can have more support if an emotional landmine comes across your path.

Summarize the brain research:

First you _____

Second you _____

Third you _____

You now have a landmine.

In your own words write an example of spank the dog:

_____

_____

_____

_____

What is the day you put a rubber band on your wrist? _____

What Scripture would you like to quote when utilizing the rubber band?

_____

_____

In your own words describe the concept of braindar:

_____

_____

_____

_____

What would it mean for you to hate well?

_____

_____

_____

_____

In your own words, describe a brain covenant.

_____

_____

_____

_____

If you felt the need to make a brain covenant, write the date you made that covenant._____

The most important things I have learned from this chapter are:

_____

_____

_____

_____

The date you shared your answers with another man was: _____

Holy Hologram

Just for grins in this chapter I shared with you one of my favorite TV shows growing up. In the below space write out one of your favorite TV shows?

_____

Why was it a favorite show?

_____

_____

_____

_____

In your own words define hologram.

_____

_____

_____

_____

In the below space, write what someone would have to say if they were describing you holographically.

_____

_____

_____

_____

In your own words, describe a woman's spirit.

_____

_____

_____

_____

In your own words, describe a woman's soul.

_____

_____

_____

_____

In your own words, describe any woman in a holographic manner.

_____

_____

_____

_____

When you hear the word holy, what images or thoughts come to mind?

1. _____

2. _____

3. _____

4. _____

5. _____

Describe why a body is innately holy.

_____

_____

_____

_____

How would the world be different if every man saw every woman as holy?

_____

_____

_____

_____

According to Isaiah 58:7, what is our responsibility when we see the naked?

_____

_____

_____

Which of the Ten Commandments do we break when we lust after another woman? Write it out here.

_____

_____

_____

What did you learn from the Scripture Habakkuk 2:15-16, about looking at nakedness and its impact on a man?

_____

_____

_____

In your own words, describe Abraham and Lot's response to the holy angels.

_____

_____

_____

_____

In your own words, describe the response of the men of Sodom to the holiness of these angels.

_____

_____

_____

_____

What is your response to the statement, "Holiness brings out who we are."?

_____

_____

_____

_____

What is your response to the statement I made, "I believe nakedness is holiness..."?

_____

_____

_____

_____

What did you learn from Canaan's response to Noah's nakedness and who it impacted?

_____

_____

_____

_____

What did you learn from Shem and Japheth's response to Noah's nakedness and who it impacted?

_____

_____

_____

_____

In your own words, what did you learn from the section of Scripture in Hosea 4?

_____

_____

_____

_____

What do you think about the positive and negative impacts your sexuality can have on your daughter or future daughter?

_____

_____

_____

_____

What are your thoughts about the statement, "You are the protector of the holiness and nakedness of women..."?

_____

_____

_____

_____

How does God feel about your current providing of protection, or lack of protection, toward women?

_____

_____

_____

_____

The most important things I have learned from this chapter are:

_____

_____

_____

_____

The date you shared your answers with another man was: _____

Really Under Authority

In this chapter we talk a lot about authority. I thought it would be interesting for you to conjure up what images and thoughts come to your mind when you hear the word authority.

Images: _____

_____

_____

Thoughts: _____

_____

_____

What is the lie most men have bought about their sex organ?

That it belongs to _____.

Take a journey with me throughout your adolescence and into manhood. How long do you believe that on one level or another you honestly believed your sex organ 100% belonged to you? Write the year you thought otherwise: _____.

Write down an explanation of what it means to be under authority.

_____

_____

_____

_____

Give at least one example when you acted under the authority of another.

_____

_____

_____

When we are under authority we are B_____.

When we are NOT under authority we are C _____.

Write down the first owner of your sex organ and why.

#1 Owner: _____

Why: _____

_____

What is the Scripture that supports the first owner of your sex organ?

_____

Write down the second owner of your sex organ and why.

#2 Owner: _____

Why: _____

_____

What is the Scripture that supports the second owner of your sex organ?

_____

How would you truly know if you are under the authority of the first owner?

_____

_____

_____

_____

How would you truly know if you are under the authority of the second owner?

_____

_____

_____

Explain the difference between asking permission versus asking forgiveness.

_____

_____

_____

_____

Which philosophy have you been utilizing (permission-under authority or forgiveness not under authority) with God and your wife?

God: _____

_____

Wife: _____

_____

Do you have a desire to be under authority in this area of your body and life? Why?

            Yes_____   No_____

Why: _____

_____

_____

As owner number three of your sex organ, what is your only duty?

_____

Contrast the kingdom of God and a democracy:

Kingdom of God: _____

_____

Democracy: _____

_____

Sexually, have you been operating more on a kingdom of God or a democracy philosophy?

Kingdom of God_____   Democracy_____

How do you know? _____

_____

_____

_____

How do you plan to make the first owner idea practical in your life?

_____

_____

_____

How do you plan to make the second owner idea practical in your life?

_____

_____

_____

_____

The most important things I have learned from this chapter are:

_____

_____

_____

_____

The date you shared your answers with another man was: _____

A Promised Land

Inheritance is a great idea. In our Western culture, inheritance means that when one or both of our parents die, we inherit some assets we didn't work for. As a teenager, my son jokingly has already asked to have our house when I'm gone.

However, inheritance in the Old Testament was quite a different concept. Based upon what you read in this chapter explain how inheritance is a different process:

_____

_____

_____

_____

What were the two things that the Israelites had to do or had to have done to them in order to inherit the Promised Land? To K _____ and be K _____.

What percentage of inheritance did the two and a half tribes receive prior to crossing the Jordan?

_____%

What did these two and a half tribes do in Joshua 4:12-13?

_____

_____

_____

_____

What would these men's behaviors be symbolic of today in our lives?

_____

_____

_____

_____

In the New Testament, what is our inheritance?

The very nature of _____.

What do we have to kill to receive our full inheritance? _____

L _____ is the absolute opposite of lust.

Most of us can relate to Joe's inner boy and inner man struggle. Verbally, give an example from your own life to another man who is also working through this guide.

Explain in your own words the concept of "pray for her."

_____

_____

_____

_____

How does God feel when we lust after women, His daughters?

1. _____

2. _____

3. _____

4. _____

5. _____

How do you think God feels when we choose not to lust after His daughters?

1. _____

2. _____

3. _____

4. _____

5. _____

The biggest battle in the church for men today is to S _____

C _____.

Explain in your own words the don't ask, don't tell policy of many churches as it relates to men's sexual issues.

_____

_____

_____

_____

Within church or church events, was there a time when a man asked you straight up about pornography, masturbation or other sexual issues?

_____

In your own words, write out what would an ask and tell policy look like:

_____

_____

_____

_____

What are the two questions you can ask to help your brothers get and stay clean?

When was _____

_____

When was _____

_____

Write down what you think the church male sexual culture would be like if
it followed an ask and tell policy.

_____

_____

_____

_____

What are your thoughts about Tom's Story?

_____

_____

_____

How can you make the ideas in this chapter practical in your life?

_____

_____

_____

_____

The most important things I have learned from this chapter are:

_____

_____

_____

_____

The date you shared your answers with another man was: _____

James and John

This chapter opens with a brief discussion about truth. Describe truth.

_____

_____

_____

_____

God is _____% for you.

When I was in Bible College, I tried a few approaches of getting free. List these here.

T _____

C _____

F _____

P _____

M _____ S _____

How many of these approaches have you attempted to get clean in the past?

_____

Describe what happens when we apply I John 1:9.

_____

_____

_____

_____

Describe how powerful the blood of Jesus is.

_____

_____

_____

_____

In the past, would you have been guilty of having more faith in your sin or in the blood of Christ? Give an example either way.

_____

_____

_____

_____

What did God tell me to do with my roommate?

_____

_____

_____

_____

Prior to reading this book, have you told anyone about sexual issues in your past or present?

Yes_____   No_____

Since reading this book, have you told anyone about sexual issues from your past or present?

Yes_____   No_____

If so, what have been the results of this?

_____

_____

_____

_____

Describe what happened to me once I started being honest with my room-mate?

_____

_____

_____

_____

Do you believe that what God did for me He will do for others that follow the same principles of honest confession to God?

Yes_____   No_____

In your own words, describe the principles in James 5:16.

_____

_____

_____

_____

Describe the difference between forgiveness and healing.

Forgiveness: _____

_____

Healing: _____

_____

Whose job is it to be responsible to confess their sin? _____

Why do men stay stuck?

P_____

Has pride been an issue for you in staying stuck in any area of your life?

     Yes_____   No_____

Give an example.

_____

_____

_____

_____

Has pride been keeping you stuck in a sexual area of your life?

     Yes_____   No_____

Give an example.

_____

_____

_____

_____

Write down James 5:16 in reverse.

_____

_____

_____

_____

What happens to a man who doesn't embrace a lifestyle of honest confession?

_____

_____

_____

_____

What are the two paths to humility?

1. _____

_____

2. _____

_____

What would be some of the characteristics of a man you would confess to?

1. _____

2. _____

3. _____

4. _____

5. _____

List the names of a few men you know that fit most of the above description.

1. _____

2. _____

3. _____

4. _____

5. _____

Describe the significance of Christ's head and body concept.

_____

_____

_____

_____

Describe the fourth and fifth reason men don't confess their sin.

Fourth: _____

_____

Fifth: _____

_____

What would your behavior have to be for you to receive both forgiveness and healing?

_____

_____

_____

_____

What have you learned from discussing the difference between John and James?

_____

_____

_____

_____

The most important things I have learned from this chapter are:

_____

_____

_____

_____

The date you shared your answers with another man was: _____

Road to Trouble

This chapter is an exposé on men who travel this road to trouble across time and geography. What is the most important thing that men have in common who travel this road?

_____

_____

_____

_____

What were some of the issues from Dewayne's adolescent and college years that could be problematic? _____

_____

_____

_____

How would you describe a marriage that is more functional than relational?

_____

_____

_____

_____

How was Dewayne at reading his Bible? What impact do you think this had on Dewayne as he traveled the road to trouble?

_____

_____

_____

_____

What were some of the factors impacting Carol at the time she and Dewayne were working together?

_____

_____

_____

_____

Describe how fantasy played a role for both Dewayne and Carol.

Dewayne: _____

_____

Carol: _____

_____

As you read Dewayne's story, what do you think was the event that was a turning point for Dewayne and Carol?

_____

_____

_____

_____

What were some of the decisions Dewayne was facing when he came to my office?

_____

_____

_____

_____

In your own words, describe the principle of "Fear God."

_____

_____

_____

What would it mean for you personally to fear God in the sexual/romantic areas of your life?

_____

_____

_____

_____

Describe in your own words the principle of being honest.

_____

_____

_____

_____

What would it mean for you to apply this principle of being honest in your life sexually and otherwise?

_____

_____

_____

Describe in your own words the principle of talking with your wife.

_____

_____

_____

_____

Are there things you need to talk to your wife about?

Yes_____   No_____

Do you need a pastor, other couple or counselor present to bring up these issues with your wife?

Yes_____   No_____

Describe not believing in a secret:

_____

_____

_____

_____

In the past, how have you believed in a secret in your sexual life?

_____

_____

_____

_____

Describe the principle of imagining the worst:

_____

_____

_____

Describe what if would look like if the worst happened and you crossed the line with another person. Who would be impacted? How could they be impacted?

_____

_____

_____

_____

_____

_____

Write down the principle of exit and entrance signs.

_____

_____

_____

_____

How can you address with your wife your need to be touched by her?

_____

_____

_____

_____

How can you address with your wife your need for praise from her?

_____

_____

_____

_____

What is going to be your rule of thumb if another woman praises you?

_____

_____

_____

What was important for you concerning the principle of respect?

_____

_____

_____

_____

Write down your thoughts on the principle of daily declarations.

_____

_____

_____

_____

If you were to have a daily declaration, write out what it would be.

_____

_____

_____

_____

What is your commitment to the prayer principle in this war?

_____

_____

_____

_____

What would it mean for you to be a hero in one story?

_____

_____

_____

_____

What do you need to do, or do differently, for you to be a hero in your one story?

_____

_____

_____

_____

The most important things I have learned from this chapter are:

_____

_____

_____

_____

The date you shared your answers with another man was: _____

Two Sided Problem

This chapter opens up with my experiences traveling and speaking around the world, and talking to men at the close of these sessions. What percentages of men, regardless of denomination or geographical location, will admit to being sexually addicted? _____%

What are your thoughts or feelings about this many men in the church having a sexual addiction?

_____

_____

_____

_____

_____

In your own words, describe each characteristic of an addiction:

Effort: _____

_____

Read My Lips: _____

_____

Consequences:_____

_____

Keeping it Going: _____

_____

Do More: _____

_____

Takes More: _____

_____

More Time: _____

_____

The Blues: _____

_____

Decreasing Other Activities: _____

_____

As you read through these characteristics, is there any area of your life that you feel you could have an addiction by having three or more of these characteristics?

Yes_____   No_____

Based upon these characteristics, do you feel you have an addiction to a sexual issue in your life?

Yes_____   No_____

If the answer is yes, how do you feel about admitting this?

_____

_____

_____

_____

I realize half of you reading this chapter do not have an issue and half do. Regardless, you will know a man who needs to know the five commandments to start walking a path of healing and recovery for himself. In light of this, I want you to write out the five commandments.

P _____

R _____

M _____

C _____

P _____

When you hear the statement, "Every church can be a hospital station for sexually addicted men in the body of Christ in their city," what thoughts or images come to your mind?

_____

_____

_____

_____

What is the definition of intimacy anorexia?

_____

_____

_____

_____

Briefly, describe each characteristic of intimacy anorexia.

Busy: _____

_____

Blame: _____

_____

Withholding Love: _____

_____

Withholding Praise: _____

_____

Withholding Sex: _____

_____

Withholding Spirituality: _____

_____

Withholding Feelings: _____

_____

Criticism: _____

_____

Anger/Silence: _____

_____

Money: _____

_____

When you took the test on what your wife would say about you, what was your yes score? _____

What did this tell you?

_____

_____

_____

_____

When you took the test regarding these characteristics about your wife, what was her yes score? _____

What did this tell you about her?

_____

_____

_____

_____

The most important things I have learned from this chapter are:

_____

_____

_____

The date you shared your answers with another man was: _____

Staying on Offense

We talk about sports in this chapter. What have been your experiences of being in a sport?

_____

_____

_____

_____

What are some of the positive things you learned from sports?

_____

_____

_____

_____

What is the prize the enemy is after in this war?

_____

_____

_____

_____

What is the first way we can change our scoreboard?

_____

_____

_____

_____

Give an example of leading a man to Christ.

_____

_____

_____

_____

If you don't have an example, what is your plan to start training yourself to lead people to Christ?

_____

_____

_____

_____

What is the second way we change the scoreboard?

_____

_____

_____

_____

How can you stay on offense with your son (if applicable)?

_____

_____

_____

_____

How can you stay on offense with your brother in Christ?

_____

_____

_____

_____

What are ideas you have to help teens stay on offense in your church?

_____

_____

_____

_____

What are ideas you have to help singles stay on offense in your church?

_____

_____

_____

What are ideas you have to help engaged couples stay on offense in your church?

_____

_____

_____

What ideas do you have to help married people stay on offense in your church?

_____

_____

_____

_____

What are the antibodies in the local church?

_____

_____

_____

_____

What images and thoughts come to your mind when you hear the statement, "You are a solution for yourself, your family, your church and our culture."?

For Yourself: _____

_____

Your Family: _____

_____

Your Church: _____

_____

Your Culture: _____

_____

As you read the story of Levi and Eli what touched you?

_____

_____

_____

_____

The most important things I have learned from this chapter are:

_____

_____

_____

_____

The date you shared your answers with another man was: _____

I honestly want to thank you and congratulate you for going through this journey. I am genuinely excited how God is going to bless and expand your life. If you have a testimony or question, my email is heart2heart@xc.org. Remember, you are truly a solution!

Douglas Weiss, Ph.D.

Appendix

MEN'S RECOVERY

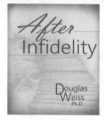

WOMEN'S RECOVERY

This book offers the readers hope, along with a plan for recovery. Any woman who is a partner of a sex addict will find this book a necessity for her journey toward healing. $14.95

This is like therapy in a box for women who want to walk through the residual effects of being in a relationship with a sex addict. $39.95

This is an interactive workbook that allows the partners of sex addicts to gain insight and strength through working the Twelve Steps. $14.95

This addresses the pain, trauma, and betrayal women experience because of their partner's sex addiction, betrayal, and/or intimacy anorexia. $29.95

This DVD provides a clear path to processing your desire for safety and creates a roadmap to reclaim safety regardless of your partner or spouse's choices. $29.95

This DVD is for every woman who has experienced the pain of their partner's sex addiction or intimacy anorexia and feels stuck, confused, frustrated and unable to move on.$29.00

This DVD set helps women accept this immature reality and gives them practical ways to navigate their husband's re-maturing process if he chooses recovery. $49.99

Your pain and betrayal are real and are addressed in this DVD series. You deserve the best answer to your questions and in just under 2 hours you can have them answered for you. $69.95

In this DVD set Dr. Weiss will expose the viewer to specific reasons as to why men lie and helpful strategies to end the lying. $44.95

INTIMACY ANOREXIA

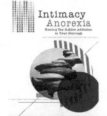

Intimacy Anorexia
Healing The Hidden Addiction
to Your Marriage

Douglas Weiss, Ph.D.

This hidden addiction is destroying so many marriages today. In your hands is the first antidote for a person or spouse with anorexia to turn the pages on this addiction process. $22.95

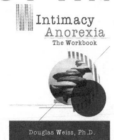

Intimacy Anorexia
The Workbook

Douglas Weiss, Ph.D.

This is like therapy in a box. Inside is 100 exercises that have already been proven helpful in treating intimacy anorexia. $39.95

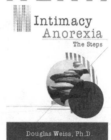

Intimacy Anorexia
The Steps

Douglas Weiss, Ph.D.

This is the only twelve step workbook just for intimacy anorexia. Each step gives you progress in your healing from intimacy anorexia. $14.95

This book will not only unlock the understanding of intimacy anorexia but you will also hear experiences of spouses who have found themselves married and alone. $14.95

This is the first workbook to offer practical suggestions and techniques to better navigate through recovery from your spouse's Intimacy Anorexia. $39.95

These Steps can further your healing and recovery from your spouse's Intimacy Anorexia. $14.95

This DVD will give you the characteristics, causes and strategies of intimacy anorexia. This DVD also provides solutions for the intimacy anorexic to start their road to recovery. $69.95

This DVD is for the spouse of an intimacy/sexual anorexic. Dr. Weiss will help you to start a journey of recovery from living with a spouse with intimacy anorexia. $49.95

Dr. Weiss has put together the eight reasons why couples might be sexless and married as well as solutions for each reason for sexlessness. $49.95

w w w . d r d o u g w e i s s . c o m   7 1 9 . 2 7 8 . 3 7 0 8

OTHER RESOURCES

"Born for War" teaches practical tools to defeat these sexual landmines and offers scriptural truths that empower young men to desire successfulness in the war thrust upon them. $29.95

This 2 hour DVD helps single women ages 15-30, to successfully navigate through the season of dating. $29.95

This 2 Disc DVD Series is definitely nothing you have heard before. Dr. Weiss charts new territory as to the why for sexual purity. $29.95

A gift for your daugher as she enters college. Letters to my Daughter includes my daily letters to my daughter during her first year of college. $14.95

Erin discovers she comes from a long line of dragons, dragons who have effectively maintained Earth's balance since the planet's beginning. Will she accept her fate and responsibility? $14.95

Within these pages of this book you will find a tried and true path for recovery from any addiction. Here you will get a biblical understanding to break the strongholds in your life forever. $22.95

This workbook provides tips, biblical principles, techniques, and assignments that Dr. Weiss has given his addicted clients with any addiction for over twenty-five years. $39.95

These steps were derived from a Christian perspective and offer much needed insight and practical wisdom to help you get free and stay free from any addiction. $14.95

This Dvd series includes leadership training and fifty segments that are about 10 minutes in length. Churches of any size can begin a Recovery for Everyone group in their local church. $99.00

Men Make Men

Dr. Weiss takes the listeners by the hand and step-by-step walks through the creative process God used to make every man into a man of God. This practical teaching on DVD combined with the Men Make Guidebook can revitalize the men in any home or local church. DVD - $29.95 GUIDE BOOK - $11.95

Worthy

This Series is designed for anyone who has struggled with doubting their amazing worth. This insightful and pragmatic journey to worthy is one every believer should experience. You are worth this journey to see what others see - your worth! $29.95

Worthy Exercise & Step book {all in one}

This workbook has been a labor of love. I have seen countless people move from a lifestyle of worthlessness to worthy, and their lives have inspired me to write this. What you have here is a path that anyone can take to get and stay worthy. Follow this path, and you too will make the journey from worthless to worthy, just as others have. $29.95

COUNSELING

"Without the intensive, my marriage would have ended and I would not have known why. Now I am happier than ever and my marriage is bonded permanently."

Counseling Sessions

Couples are helped through critical phases of disclosure moving into the process of recovery, and rebuilding trust in relationships. We have helped many couples rebuild their relationship and grasp and implement the necessary skills for an intimate relationship.

Individual counseling offers a personal treatment plan for successful healing in your life. In just one session a counselor can help you understand how you became stuck and how to move toward freedom.

Partners of sex addicts need an advocate. Feelings of fear, hurt, anger, betrayal, and grief require a compassionate, effective response. We provide that expert guidance and direction. We have helped many partners heal through sessions that get them answers to their many questions including: "How can I trust him again?"

A counseling session today can begin your personal journey toward healing.

3 and 5 Day Intensives

in Colorado Springs, Colorado
are available for the following issues:

- Sexual Addiction
- Marriage
- Pastors
- Partners of Sexual Addicts
- Intimacy Anorexia
- Victims of Sexual Abuse
- Adult Children of Sex Addicts
- Teenage Children of Sex Addicts
- Teens

Attendees of Intensives will receive:

- Personal attention from counselors who specialize in your area of need

- An understanding of how the addiction /anorexia and its consequences came into being

- Three counseling sessions daily

- Daily assignments to increase the productiveness of these daily sessions

- Individuals get effective counseling to recover from the effects of sexual addiction, abuse and intimacy anorexia.

- Addiction, abuse, anorexia issues are thoroughly addressed for couples and individuals. This includes the effects on the partner or family members of the addict, and how to rebuild intimacy toward a stronger relationship.

A·A·S·A·T

American Association for Sex Addiction Therapy

Cost: $795

Both male and female clinicians are desiring to counsel sexually addictive behaviors more than ever. You can be prepared! Forty-eight hours of topics related to sexual addiction treatment are covered in this training including:

- The Six Types of Sex Addicts
- Sex and Recovery
- Case Assessment
- Behavior Treatment Plans for each type

- Neurological Understanding
- Relapse Strategies
- Comorbidity Issues
- Intimacy Anorexia

Cost: $595

With this AASAT training, you will gain proven clinical insight into treating the issues facing partners of sex addicts. You can be prepared! Over thirty hours of topics related to partners treatment are covered in this training, including:

- Partner Model
- Anger
- Partners as Intimacy Anorexics
- Separation

- Partner Grief
- Boundaries
- Reactive Intimacy Anorexia
- Polygraph Questions

Cost: $695

This is the only available training to become certified to treat Intimacy Anorexia. Dr. Weiss developed this training program utilizing his own, proven methodology and modality as well as his clinical application for treatment.

This growing issue of Intimacy Anorexia will need your competent help in your community. Now, you can be prepared to identify it and treat it. In this training you'll cover topics like:

- Identifying Intimacy Anorexia
- Comorbid Issues
- Relapse Strategies
- Characteristics of Intimacy Anorexia

- Causes of Intimacy Anorexia
- Treatment Plan
- Marital Treatment
- Sexual Recovery Issues

For More Information:
Call 719.330.2425 or visit www.aasat.org

amazon.com®

If you have found this book helpful, please
take a moment and review it on Amazon.

Thanks, Dr. Doug